AF365637

Self-Righteous Poetry

Hannah Hulett-Pugh

BookLeaf Publishing

India | USA | UK

Copyright © Hannah Hulett-Pugh

All Rights Reserved.

This book has been self-published with all reasonable efforts taken to make the material error-free by the author. No part of this book shall be used, reproduced in any manner whatsoever without written permission from the author, except in the case of brief quotations embodied in critical articles and reviews.

The Author of this book is solely responsible and liable for its content including but not limited to the views, representations, descriptions, statements, information, opinions, and references ["Content"]. The Content of this book shall not constitute or be construed or deemed to reflect the opinion or expression of the Publisher or Editor. Neither the Publisher nor Editor endorse or approve the Content of this book or guarantee the reliability, accuracy, or completeness of the Content published herein and do not make any representations or warranties of any kind, express or implied, including but not limited to the implied warranties of merchantability, fitness for a particular purpose.

The Publisher and Editor shall not be liable whatsoever...

Made with ❤ on the BookLeaf Publishing Platform

www.bookleafpub.in

www.bookleafpub.com

Dedication

*For my babies, who keep me rooted and my husband,
who keeps me grounded.*
Love always, Mommy

Preface

Because it's only ideation,
Until you act on it,
And then what is it,
If not but too late.

- HHP

Acknowledgements

Approximately 23.1% of adult Americans suffer from some form of mental illness and approximately 26.9% of Americans 12 and older struggle with substance or alcohol abuse.

For the Missouri Fam

You can call or text 988 to reach the 988 Suicide & Crisis Lifeline for mental health, suicide, or substance use crises. You can also chat with a crisis counselor online at chat.988lifeline.org.

For Friends Outside of Missouri

National Suicide Prevention Lifeline 1-800-273-TALK(8255)

SAMHSA's National Helpline, 1-800-662-HELP (4357) (also known as the Treatment Referral Routing Service), or TTY: 1-800-487-4889 is a confidential, free, 24-hour-a-day, 365-day-a-year, information service, in English and Spanish, for individuals and family members facing mental and/or substance use disorders. This service provides referrals to local treatment facilities, support

groups, and community-based organizations.
Also visit the online treatment locator, or send your zip code via text message: 435748 (HELP4U) to find help near you.
As per https://www.samhsa.gov/find-help/helplines/national-helpline

Know that help is available to you and I'm rooting for you.

The Chair is Empty

The chair is empty, the laughter's gone,
A silent room, a hollow dawn.
Your note, a whisper, a final plea,
A pain too deep for me to see.

We walked through fields of joy and strife,
Two souls entwined, a shared life.
Now memories flicker, a fading flame,
And all that's left is your whispered name.

I search for answers in the gray,
Why did you choose to go this way?
The world feels colder, the colors dim,
A broken chord, a mournful hymn.

Though darkness lingers, I'll hold on tight,
To fragments of your fading light.
And in the silence, I will try,
To find a way to say goodbye.

Where Shadows Sleep

The veil is thin, the air grows cold,
A whisper chills down to the bone.
The world I know, a story told,
Fades swiftly as I'm left alone.

No stars above, no moonlit sky,
Just swirling mists of inky black.
Where shadows dance and spirits fly,
And there's no turning, no way back.

The ground gives way to shifting sand,
A barren land of endless night.
With outstretched hand and trembling stance,
I stumble on in fading light.

Twisted trees with branches bare,
Reach out like claws in silent plea.
Their gnarled roots, a twisted snare,
Awaiting souls like you and me.

A distant call, a haunting cry,
Echoes through this desolate space.
Lost voices wail, a mournful sigh,
Forgotten souls in endless chase.

Through fractured realms and shattered dreams,
I wander, lost in shades of gray.
Where reality is not what it seems,
And darkness holds eternal sway.

The path ahead, unknown, unseen,
Yet something calls me to the deep.
A chilling truth, a haunting scene,
In this between where shadows sleep.

She Bleeds the Stars

A silver cord, unseen, yet strong,
Woven through stardust, where they belong.
A lunar pull, a tidal sway,
Before the words, she knew the way.

Two hearts entwined, a mirrored beat,
A whispered language, bittersweet.
From cosmic depths, a soul takes flight,
Entrusted to her guiding light.

An ancient dance, a primal art,
A universe held in her heart.
Through veils of pain and ecstasy,
A sacred bond, eternally.

She is the earth, the fertile ground,
Where tiny seeds of life are found.
A whispered prayer, a lullaby,
Beneath the vast and endless sky.

She bleeds the stars, she breathes the breeze,
She calls all the cosmos to their knees.
Through joy and sorrow, fear and grace,
She holds her future in embrace.

The Sculptor

A sculptor once found a rare, luminous stone,
Perfect for carving a masterpiece, all on her own.
She dreamed of the statue, exquisite and grand,
A testament to her skill, the finest in the land.

But her child grew hungry, their small hands did reach,
For warmth and for comfort, beyond her art's preach.
The sculptor looked down, at the stone, then the child,
One promised her glory, the other, love's wild,

Unpredictable landscape, of need and of care,
A bond that demanded a sacrifice rare.
She put down her chisel, her dream put on hold,
And gathered her child, shielding them from the cold.

Years passed in a blur, of laughter and tears,
Of scraped knees and stories, that banished all fears.
The stone lay forgotten, in a corner, unseen,
As the sculptor poured love, where her ambition had
been.

One day, the child, now grown, strong, and bright,
Found the stone, dusty, yet bathed in soft light.
"Mother," they asked, "what treasure is this, you see?"

She smiled, "A dream I once had, before you chose me.

But the greatest creation a mother can claim,
Is not carved from stone, nor whispered in fame.
It's the love that she gives, the life she helps grow,"
And in her child's eyes, she saw her heart's glow,
A masterpiece sculpted, not by chisel or art,
But by the boundless devotion, of a mother's own heart.

Lucid Dreaming

Suicidal but in like a platonic way, ya know?
Cause like I got kids and shit so,
Call me Marilyn,
But know that my ex did it.

In Regard to Oral

She had heard of performing the alphabet but she didn't know about the symphonies to come.

Mosaic Scars

The shattered vase, a love betrayed,
Sharp shards of trust, a heart flayed.
Promises broken, a whispered lie,
Tears like rivers, running dry.

The fractured bond, a gaping wound,
Where whispers of doubt deeply resound.
Forgiveness falters, anger ignites,
A battle within, day and through nights.

But from the ashes, embers glow,
A flicker of hope, starts to grow.
Through self-reflection, strength takes root,
Healing blossoms, bearing fruit.

The broken pieces, carefully gleaned,
A mosaic of love, a new scene.
Scars remain, a reminder bold,
Of a love reborn, a story told.

Though cracks may linger, a fragile art,
A stronger love, a brand new start.
Forgiving the trespass, a choice so brave,
Rebuilding trust, beyond the grave.

Masquerade of Mirth

A masquerade of mirth, a vibrant hue,
I dance among the crowd, a dazzling view.
Then shadows call, a quiet, beckoning hand,
I slip away, to a solitary land.

The energy that flowed, now gently ebbs,
A spider spinning introspective webs.
Two sides I hold, a sun and moon embrace,
A public smile, a private, hidden space.

Do I crave the stage, or silence deep and cool?
A paradox, a captivating, swirling pool.
The world perceives a flame, a burning bright,
Unknowing of the stillness, and the quiet night.

My New Best-PTSD

Oh, joy, another flashback, how grand,
Just what I needed, a trip to trauma-land.
My brain's a funhouse, mirrors all askew,
Reflecting back the hell I wandered through.

Sleep? You jest, that's for the lucky few,
My nights are filled with things I can't undo.
Loud noises, crowds, a certain shade of blue,
Triggers abound, like landmines, shining new.

"Just get over it," they chirp with obnoxious smiles,
If only healing were that easy, miles
Of therapy and meds, a constant fight,
To keep the darkness from consuming light.

So pardon me if I'm a bit on edge,
My mind's a battlefield, constantly close to the ledge.
But hey, at least I'm never bored, no not me,
Just living the dream, with my new best-PTSD.

Mental Tomb

A constant knot in my chest,
A feeling of impending doom.
My heart races, my breath catches,
I'm trapped in a mental tomb.

My thoughts spiral out of control,
Worry gnaws at my mind.
I'm restless, I'm irritable.
I'm losing my peace of mind.

I try to hide it, but it's always there.
In my eyes, in my smile,
A constant companion, a heavy weight,
That drags me down for a mile.

I know I'm not alone,
That others feel this way.
But that doesn't make it easier,
To face each anxious day.

Tiny Tyrant

The clock strikes three, the hour is late,
A tiny tyrant seals my fate.
No peaceful slumber, no respite in sight,
Just piercing cries throughout the night.

The day unfolds in a blur of fatigue,
A whirlwind of needs, a constant besiege.
Coffee grows cold, ambitions take flight,
Replaced by the duties of day and of night.

Yet amidst the chaos, a truth softly gleams,
A love so profound, it surpasses all dreams.
In tiny smiles and fingers so small,
A bond unbreakable, encompassing all.

Anxious Bird

My heart's a hummingbird on espresso,
A trapped moth in a disco.
Thoughts race like a runaway train,
Derailing again and again.

My breath, a hiccup in the throat,
A tightrope walker with no coat.
The world's a funhouse mirror's gaze,
Distorting everything always.

But hey, at least I'll die tired,
If I don't spontaneously combust first, I'm a liar.
So cheers to anxiety, my frenemy,
Making sure I never rest easy.

Not Supposed To Be

You're not supposed to be pale white,
But you're also not supposed to be black either.
You're supposed to be that pretty caramel color
That falls somewhere in the middle,
But God forbid you be Latino.

You're supposed to be skinny,
But not too skinny so that your ribs show.
You're supposed to have a big butt and big boobs,
But forget having any kind of stomach in between.

Apparently we should just start
Surgically removing the middle section of our bodies
And pop her tits right down on her ass.
Walk around like some kind a fucked up duck
Because at least then,

Our legs would look longer.

Arbitrary Goals

Be thin but curvy, a walking dream,
An hourglass figure, it would seem.
No cellulite, no stretch marks, please,
Smooth as plastic, if you seize

The chance to starve and sculpt and squeeze.
Your waist must be a tiny vine,
Your breasts? Perky, plump, and fine.
Forget the bones, the skin, the soul,

Just reach that arbitrary goal.
And if you fail? Don't you fret,
There's filters for that, you can bet.
So chase the phantom, taut and trim,
This beauty game? You'll never win.

Dramatic Dragons

In the cavern of my soul, resides
A rather dramatic dragon, who presides
Over a hoard of worries, big and small,
Ready to torch my sanity, standing tall.

Most days he snoozes, grumpy, gassy, curled,
A rumbling threat to my internal world.
But poke him with a deadline, or a doubt,
And watch the flames of panic spout.

He's got a flair for the theatrical, see,
One whiff of stress? "Oh, woe is me!"
He roars and thrashes, breathes a fiery fit,
"The sky is falling! We're all doomed, I say, this is it!"

I've tried negotiations, logic, and deep breaths,
To quell his angst, to soothe his fiery breaths.
Sometimes it works, he'll grumble, then retreat,
Muttering, "Fine, but I still smell defeat!"

So I tiptoe 'round, this beast of anxious might,
Hoping he stays asleep, and out of sight.
But life, alas, is full of pokes and prods,
So I'll go to meet the dragon, that's the odds.

Endless Night

Death, a specter, forever lingers near,
In life's fleeting moments, he's always here.
His skeletal hand, a chilling embrace,
Stealing vitality, leaving no trace.

He favors no man, rich or poor the same,
A macabre jester in life's grand game.
With hollow eyes and a skeletal grin,
He stalks his prey, an inevitable win.

But fear him not, nor succumb to despair,
Embrace life's flame, let your spirit flare.
For Death is a chapter, a destined plight,
A transition to the endless night.

Clockwork Moon

The clockwork moon hangs in the velvet sky,
A silver cog in an endless drive,
Stars like diamonds scattered nigh,
Where silent shadows softly thrive.

A whispering wind through rusted trees,
Carries secrets on its breath,
Of forgotten dreams and memories,
Lost in the undergrowth of death.

A lone wolf howls at the lunar face,
A mournful cry in the still of night,
Echoes ripple through time and space,
A lonely soul in fading light.

The world sleeps on, oblivious and deep,
To the mysteries that the darkness keep.
And still the clockwork moon wanes on,
A carousel that doesn't halt for anyone.

Monochrome Demons

The world was a monochrome canvas,
A silent film with no laughter.
Each day, a heavy anchor,
Dragging me down, down, under.

The mirror showed a stranger,
Eyes hollow, smile a ghost.
Apathy, my constant ranger,
Guiding me to a barren coast.

Sleep was a seductive temptress,
Offering oblivion's embrace.
Wakefulness, a cruel mistress,
With a whip and a mocking face.

But somewhere within the darkness,
A tiny spark refused to die.
A flicker of defiance, a rebellious starkness,
Against the overwhelming lie.

I stumbled, I faltered, I fell,
But each time, I clawed my way back.
I fought against the siren's spell,
And reclaimed my own track.

The colors seeped back in slowly,
The laughter returned in hesitant bursts.
The world was no longer wholly
A desolate land of the worst.

It's a journey, not a destination,
This fight against the inner demons.
But with each step, a liberation,
A reclaiming of my own reasons.

Paint Me with the Void

24

A silent bloom, a lotus in the mind,
Unfolding petals, leaving self behind.
A mirror shattered, reflections cease to be,
Only the vastness of eternity.

A whisper echoes, from a timeless shore,
"You are the wave, and you are the ocean's roar."
No striving now, no path left to pursue,
The seeker vanished, leaving only You.

A boundless canvas, painted with the void,
Where no atom is ever annoyed.
In this great stillness, peace begins to flow,
The quiet knowing that you already know.

The Weaver

A weaver had a tapestry, a vibrant, loving art,
Woven with threads of joy and trust, a masterpiece to
start.
But storms arose, and threads grew frayed, the colors
lost their hue,
A careless word, a thoughtless act, the fabric tore in two.

His neighbor saw the tattered cloth, and whispered in his
ear,
"Discard this wreck, it's far too gone, and weave a new
one, dear.
This tapestry's beyond repair, its beauty's lost to time,
Begin anew, with brighter threads, a more harmonious
rhyme."

The weaver wept, he almost gave, to sorrow's heavy
hand,
But then he saw a single thread, still shining in the
strand.
A memory of laughter shared, a promise whispered low,
He knelt and touched the fragile thread, and felt a gentle
glow.

With patient hands, and loving heart, he started to repair,
Each broken thread, a lesson learned, a burden he would bear.
He sought out new, resilient strands, of patience, trust, and grace,
And slowly, slowly, wove them in, to fill the empty space.

The work was hard, the nights were long, his fingers ached and bled,
But with each knot, the tapestry, a stronger pattern spread.
The colors bloomed, more vibrant now, than ever they had been,
A testament to love's enduring power, a victory hard-won.

So let this be a lesson learned, for hearts that start to fray,
A marriage, like a tapestry, can find a brighter day.
Don't cast aside the threads of love, when storms begin to brew,
But fight to mend, with gentle hands, and make it strong and new.